CONFEDERATE BLOOD AND TREASURE

THE LOCHLAINN SEABROOK COLLECTION

AMERICAN CIVIL WAR
Abraham Lincoln Was a Liberal, Jefferson Davis Was a Conservative: The Missing Key to Understanding the American Civil War
Confederacy 101: Amazing Facts You Never Knew About America's Oldest Political Tradition
Confederate Blood and Treasure: An Interview With Lochlainn Seabrook
Everything You Were Taught About African-Americans and the Civil War is Wrong, Ask a Southerner!
Everything You Were Taught About the Civil War is Wrong, Ask a Southerner!
Give This Book to a Yankee! A Southern Guide to the Civil War For Northerners
Heroes of the Southern Confederacy: The Illustrated Book of Confederate Officials, Soldiers, and Civilians
Lincoln's War: The Real Cause, the Real Winner, the Real Loser
The Great Yankee Coverup: What the North Doesn't Want You to Know About Lincoln's War!
The Ultimate Civil War Quiz Book: How Much Do You Really Know About America's Most Misunderstood Conflict?
Women in Gray: A Tribute to the Ladies Who Supported the Southern Confederacy

CONFEDERATE MONUMENTS
Confederate Monuments: Why Every American Should Honor Confederate Soldiers and Their Memorials

CONFEDERATE FLAG
Confederate Flag Facts: What Every American Should Know About Dixie's Southern Cross
What the Confederate Flag Means to Me: Americans Speak Out in Defense of Southern Honor, Heritage, and History

SECESSION
All We Ask Is To Be Let Alone: The Southern Secession Fact Book

SLAVERY
Everything You Were Taught About American Slavery is Wrong, Ask a Southerner!
Slavery 101: Amazing Facts You Never Knew About America's "Peculiar Institution"

CHILDREN
Honest Jeff and Dishonest Abe: A Southern Children's Guide to the Civil War
Saddle, Sword, and Gun: A Biography of Nathan Bedford Forrest For Teens

NATHAN BEDFORD FORREST
A Rebel Born: A Defense of Nathan Bedford Forrest - Confederate General, American Legend (winner of the 2011 Jefferson Davis Historical Gold Medal)
A Rebel Born: The Screenplay (film about N. B. Forrest)
Forrest! 99 Reasons to Love Nathan Bedford Forrest
Give 'Em Hell Boys! The Complete Military Correspondence of Nathan Bedford Forrest
I Rode With Forrest! Confederate Soldiers Who Served With the World's Greatest Cavalry Leader
Nathan Bedford Forrest and African-Americans: Yankee Myth, Confederate Fact
Nathan Bedford Forrest and the Battle of Fort Pillow: Yankee Myth, Confederate Fact
Nathan Bedford Forrest and the Ku Klux Klan: Yankee Myth, Confederate Fact
Nathan Bedford Forrest: Southern Hero, American Patriot - Honoring a Confederate Icon and the Old South
Saddle, Sword, and Gun: A Biography of Nathan Bedford Forrest For Teens
The God of War: Nathan Bedford Forrest As He Was Seen By His Contemporaries
The Quotable Nathan Bedford Forrest: Selections From the Writings and Speeches of the Confederacy's Most Brilliant Cavalryman

QUOTABLE SERIES
The Alexander H. Stephens Reader: Excerpts From the Works of a Confederate Founding Father
The Quotable Alexander H. Stephens: Selections From the Writings and Speeches of the Confederacy's First Vice President
The Quotable Jefferson Davis: Selections From the Writings and Speeches of the Confederacy's First President
The Quotable Nathan Bedford Forrest: Selections From the Writings and Speeches of the Confederacy's Most Brilliant Cavalryman
The Quotable Robert E. Lee: Selections From the Writings and Speeches of the South's Most Beloved Civil War General
The Quotable Stonewall Jackson: Selections From the Writings and Speeches of the South's Most Famous General
The Unquotable Abraham Lincoln: The President's Quotes They Don't Want You To Know!

CIVIL WAR BATTLES
Encyclopedia of the Battle of Franklin - A Comprehensive Guide to the Conflict that Changed the Civil War
Nathan Bedford Forrest and the Battle of Fort Pillow: Yankee Myth, Confederate Fact
The Battle of Franklin: Recollections of Confederate and Union Soldiers
The Battle of Nashville: Recollections of Confederate and Union Soldiers
The Battle of Spring Hill: Recollections of Confederate and Union Soldiers

CONSTITUTIONAL HISTORY
America's Three Constitutions: Complete Texts of the Articles of Confederation, Constitution of the United States of America, and Constitution of the Confederate States of America
The Articles of Confederation Explained: A Clause-by-Clause Study of America's First Constitution
The Constitution of the Confederate States of America Explained: A Clause-by-Clause Study of the South's Magna Carta

VICTORIAN CONFEDERATE LITERATURE
I, Confederate: Why the South Seceded and Fought in the Words of 19th-Century Southerners
Rise Up and Call Them Blessed: Victorian Tributes to the Confederate Soldier, 1861-1901
Support Your Local Confederate: Wit and Humor in the Southern Confederacy
The Bittersweet Bond: Race Relations in the Old South as Described by White and Black Southerners
The God of War: Nathan Bedford Forrest As He Was Seen By His Contemporaries
The Old Rebel: Robert E. Lee As He Was Seen By His Contemporaries
Victorian Confederate Poetry: The Southern Cause in Verse, 1861-1901

ABRAHAM LINCOLN
Abraham Lincoln: The Southern View - Demythologizing America's Sixteenth President
Lincolnology: The Real Abraham Lincoln Revealed in His Own Words - A Study of Lincoln's Suppressed, Misinterpreted, and Forgotten Writings and Speeches
Lincoln's War: The Real Cause, the Real Winner, the Real Loser
The Great Impersonator! 99 Reasons to Dislike Abraham Lincoln
The Unholy Crusade: Lincoln's Legacy of Destruction in the American South
The Unquotable Abraham Lincoln: The President's Quotes They Don't Want You To Know!

NATURAL HISTORY
North America's Amazing Mammals: An Encyclopedia for the Whole Family
The Concise Book of Owls: A Guide to Nature's Most Mysterious Birds
The Concise Book of Tigers: A Guide to Nature's Most Remarkable Cats

PARANORMAL
Carnton Plantation Ghost Stories: True Tales of the Unexplained from Tennessee's Most Haunted Civil War House!
UFOs and Aliens: The Complete Guidebook

FAMILY HISTORIES
The Blakeneys: An Etymological, Ethnological, and Genealogical Study - Uncovering the Mysterious Origins of the Blakeney Family and Name
The Caudills: An Etymological, Ethnological, and Genealogical Study - Exploring the Name and National Origins of a European-American Family
The McGavocks of Carnton Plantation: A Southern History - Celebrating One of Dixie's Most Noble Confederate Families and Their Tennessee Home

MIND, BODY, SPIRIT
Autobiography of a Non-Yogi: A Scientist's Journey From Hinduism to Christianity (Dr. Amitava Dasgupta, with Lochlainn Seabrook)
Britannia Rules: Goddess-Worship in Ancient Anglo-Celtic Society - An Academic Look at the United Kingdom's Matricentric Spiritual Past
Christ Is All and In All: Rediscovering Your Divine Nature and the Kingdom Within
Christmas Before Christianity: How the Birthday of the "Sun" Became the Birthday of the "Son"
Jesus and the Gospel of Q: Christ's Pre-Christian Teachings As Recorded in the New Testament
Jesus and the Law of Attraction: The Bible-Based Guide to Creating Perfect Health, Wealth, and Happiness Following Christ's Simple Formula
Seabrook's Bible Dictionary of Traditional and Mystical Christian Doctrines
Sea Raven Press Blank Page Journal: For Reflections, Notes, and Sketches
The Bible and the Law of Attraction: 99 Teachings of Jesus, the Apostles, and the Prophets
The Book of Kelle: An Introduction to Goddess-Worship and the Great Celtic Mother-Goddess Kelle, Original Blessed Lady of Ireland
The Goddess Dictionary of Words and Phrases: Introducing a New Core Vocabulary for the Women's Spirituality Movement
The Martian Anomalies: A Photographic Search for Intelligent Life on Mars
Victorian Hernia Cures: Nonsurgical Self-Treatment of Inguinal Hernia
Vintage Southern Cookbook: 2,000 Delicious Dishes From Dixie

WOMEN
Aphrodite's Trade: The Hidden History of Prostitution Unveiled
Princess Diana: Modern Day Moon-Goddess - A Psychoanalytical and Mythological Look at Diana Spencer's Life, Marriage, and Death (with Dr. Jane Goldberg)
Women in Gray: A Tribute to the Ladies Who Supported the Southern Confederacy

REPRINTS
A Short History of the Confederate States of America (author Jefferson Davis; editor Lochlainn Seabrook)
Prison Life of Jefferson Davis (author John J. Craven; editor Lochlainn Seabrook)
Life of Beethoven (author Ludwig Nohl; editor Lochlainn Seabrook)
The New Revelation (author Arthur Conan Doyle; editor Lochlainn Seabrook)

Lochlainn Seabrook does not author books for fame and fortune, but for the love of writing and sharing his knowledge.

SeaRavenPress.com

CONFEDERATE BLOOD AND TREASURE

An Interview With Lochlainn Seabrook

Excerpted from the book, *Questions From the North; Answers From the South*, by James R. Elstad

LOCHLAINN SEABROOK

JEFFERSON DAVIS HISTORICAL GOLD MEDAL WINNER

Diligently Researched and Generously Illustrated
by the Author for the Elucidation of the Reader

2015

Sea Raven Press, Nashville, Tennessee, USA

CONFEDERATE BLOOD AND TREASURE

Published by
Sea Raven Press, Cassidy Ravensdale, President
Nashville, Tennessee, USA
SeaRavenPress.com

UNIQUE BOOKS & GIFTS FOR THE WHOLE FAMILY!

Copyright © text and illustrations Lochlainn Seabrook 2015, 2021, 2022
in accordance with U.S. and international copyright laws and regulations, as stated and protected under the Berne Union for the Protection of Literary and Artistic Property (Berne Convention), and the Universal Copyright Convention (the UCC). All rights reserved under the Pan-American and International Copyright Conventions.

PRINTING HISTORY
• 1st SRP paperback ed., 1st printing, July 2015; 2nd SRP paperback ed., 1st printing, November 2021;
2nd SRP paperback ed., 2nd printing, July 2022; ISBN: 978-0-9913779-9-2
• 1st SRP hardcover edition, 1st printing, November 2021; 2nd printing, July 2022; ISBN: 978-1-955351-13-3

ISBN: 978-0-9913779-9-2 (paperback)
Library of Congress Control Number: 2021950965

This work is the copyrighted intellectual property of Lochlainn Seabrook and has been registered with the Copyright Office at the Library of Congress in Washington, D.C., USA. No part of this work (including text, covers, drawings, photos, illustrations, maps, images, diagrams, etc.), in whole or in part, may be used, reproduced, stored in a retrieval system, or transmitted, in any form or by any means now known or hereafter invented, without written permission from the publisher. The sale, duplication, hire, lending, copying, digitalization, or reproduction of this material, in any manner or form whatsoever, is also prohibited, and is a violation of federal, civil, and digital copyright law, which provides severe civil and criminal penalties for any violations.

Confederate Blood and Treasure: An Interview With Lochlainn Seabrook, by Lochlainn Seabrook. Includes an introduction, illustrations, and suggested reading. (Interview excerpted with permission from the book, *Questions From the North; Answers From the South*, by James R. Elstad.)

ARTWORK
Front and back cover design and art, book design, layout, font selection, and interior art by Lochlainn Seabrook
All images, image captions, graphic design, and graphic art copyright © Lochlainn Seabrook
All images selected, placed, manipulated, cleaned, colored, tinted, and/or created by Lochlainn Seabrook
Cover image and design by Lochlainn Seabrook copyright ©
Cover photo, Confederate battery, Fort Johnson, with Fort Sumter in the background, Charleston, South Carolina, USA, circa 1865: George N. Barnard (1819-1902)

> All persons who approve of the authority and principles of Colonel Lochlainn Seabrook's literary work, and realize its benefits as a means of reeducating the world about the South and the Confederacy, are hereby requested to avidly recommend his books to others and to vigorously cooperate in extending their reach, scope, and influence around the globe.

The views documented in this book concerning the War for Southern Independence are those of the publisher.

WRITTEN, DESIGNED, PUBLISHED   IN THE UNITED STATES OF AMERICA

To my Confederate sires.

The most important thing people did for me was to expose me to new things.

Dr. Temple Grandin

CONTENTS

Notes to the Reader - 11
Introduction, by the Publisher - 13
The Interview - 17
Suggested Reading - 47
Meet the Interviewee - 51
Learn More - 53

"Books invite all; they constrain none."
Hartley Burr Alexander (1873-1939)

NOTES TO THE READER
by Cochlainn Seabrook

☛ In any study of America's antebellum, bellum, and postbellum periods, it is vitally important to understand that in 1860 the two major political parties—the Democrats and the newly formed Republicans—were the opposite of what they are today. In other words, the Democrats of the mid 19th Century were Conservatives, akin to the Republican Party of today, while the Republicans of the mid 19th Century were Liberals, akin to the Democratic Party of today. Thus the Confederacy's Democratic president, Jefferson Davis, was a Conservative (with libertarian leanings); the Union's Republican president, Abraham Lincoln, was a Liberal (with socialist leanings). For more on this topic see my book, *Abraham Lincoln Was a Liberal, Jefferson Davis Was a Conservative: The Missing Key to Understanding the American Civil War*.

☛ As I heartily dislike the phrase "Civil War," its use throughout this book (as well as in my other works) is worthy of an explanation.

Today America's entire literary system refers to the conflict of 1861 using the Northern term the "Civil War," whether we in the South like it or not. Thus, as all book searches by readers, libraries, and retail outlets are now performed online, and as all bookstores categorize works from this period under the heading "Civil War," book publishers and authors who deal with this particular topic have little choice but to use this term themselves. If I were to refuse to use it, as some of my Southern colleagues have suggested, few people would ever find or read my books.

Add to this the fact that scarcely any non-Southerners have ever heard of the names we in the South use for the conflict, such as the "War for Southern Independence"—or my personal preference, "Lincoln's War." It only makes sense then to use the term "Civil War" in most commercial situations.

We should also bear in mind that while today educated persons, particularly educated Southerners, all share an abhorrence for the phrase "Civil War," it was not always so. Confederates who lived through and even fought in the conflict regularly used the term throughout the 1860s, and even long after. Among them were Confederate generals such as Nathan Bedford Forrest, Richard Taylor, and Joseph E. Johnston, not to mention the Confederacy's vice president, Alexander H. Stephens. Even the Confederacy's highest leader, President Jefferson Davis, used the term "Civil War," and in one case at least, as late as 1881—the year he wrote his brilliant exposition, *The Rise and Fall of the Confederate Government*.

☛ Lincoln's War on the American people and the Constitution can never be fully understood without a thorough knowledge of the South's perspective of the conflict. For those seeking to learn the whole truth about the "Civil War," see my books, listed on pages 2 and 3. These contain footnotes and source material that could not be included in my interview in *Confederate Blood and Treasure*.

The South's greatest leader, Conservative Democrat and Secretary of War under U.S. President Franklin Pierce, Confederate President Jefferson Davis.

INTRODUCTION

Novelist James Elstad's interview with our author-historian Lochlainn Seabrook transpired between March and July 2015, the former month in which Elstad began work on his book, *Questions From the North; Answers From the South*.

Earlier, while doing research, he came into contact with numerous non-Southerners whose questions revealed an appalling ignorance of the facts behind the War for Southern Independence.

Elstad, a Copperhead, answered their enquiries, but soon realized that these answers might be better coming from Southerners themselves, and that these responses would make an excellent book.

It was at this time that he began reaching out to some of his Southern friends and contacts, one of whom was Col. Seabrook. This colorful little booklet, a brief but compelling primer concerning the South's many sacrifices in "Confederate blood and treasure," is the result of that connection.

The Publisher
Nashville, Tennessee, USA
July 2015

THE INTERVIEW

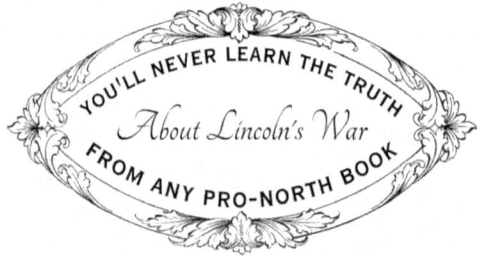

An Interview With Award-Winning Author and Civil War Scholar

LOCHLAINN SEABROOK

Conducted by James Ralph Elstad
March 2015

ELSTAD: What role did your ancestors play in Mr. Lincoln's War?

SEABROOK: I have far too many Confederate ancestors and relations to list here. However, one stands out: my third great-grandfather Elias Jent Sr., who fought in the Thirteenth Cavalry Kentucky, C.S.A., under my second cousin, Colonel Benjamin E. Caudill.

While on leave at his home in Knott County, Elias and his wife Rachel Cornett (both unarmed) were violently apprehended and hanged from a tree in their front yard by a unit of Yankee soldiers, in full view of horrified family members. This illegal and heinous execution reverberates in my family down into the present day.

ELSTAD: What was your family's station in life prior to the Civil War?

SEABROOK: I'm the sixth great-grandson of the Earl of Oxford, who settled in antebellum Virginia. These particular ancestors were part of the Southern landed gentry and were wealthy descendants of European royalty.

Most of my 19th-Century forebears, however, were everyday farmers, coal miners, and trainmen. We have a few antebellum sheriffs and outlaws in our family tree as well.

ELSTAD: Why do Southerners keep fighting the Civil War over and over?

SEABROOK: This is just another Yankee myth meant to try and obscure the truth of the matter. We Southerners are indeed still fighting, but obviously not the War itself. What we *are* doing is struggling to achieve the one and only goal that our conservative Confederate ancestors fought and died for: strict constitutionalism, which in turn infers a small limited central government, states' rights, and personal liberty.

This question should more properly be directed at the North which, though she got her way on April 9, 1865, continues to harass, belittle, attack, and criticize the South, her people, her history, her honor, and her heritage 150 years later. For what purpose? It's the same Yankee callousness and mean-spiritedness that helped lead the two countries into war to begin with.

So we continue to repeat what our Victorian Southern ancestors told their meddling neighbors to the North: "Leave us alone and mind your own business." This is something, however, that seems impossible for the naturally nosy, dictatorial Yankee. And so our plea falls on deaf ears.

Clearly it is Northerners who want to "keep fighting the Civil War over and over."

ELSTAD: The North believes that the South was responsible for the institution of slavery. How do you respond to this?

The Third Battle of Winchester (known to Yanks as the Battle of Opequon Creek) on September 19, 1864, pitted Confederate General Jubal A. Early against Union General Philip Sheridan—in the South still widely held to be one of the War's most brutal war criminals. Though the North won, it was at great cost, with some 5,000 Union casualties alone. Due to the size of the forces, the amount of bloodshed, and the overall results, Winchester III is ranked as a Class A battle, and the most significant conflict in the Shenandoah Valley.

The Battle of Five Forks on April 1, 1865, matched Confederate General George Pickett with Union General Philip Sheridan, ending in some 7,000 casualties and a Yankee win. Overwhelmed by raw numbers, the Confederacy had only days left.

SEABROOK: Another piece of false pro-North propaganda. England imposed slavery on the American North and Yankees imposed it on the American South. In fact, the American slave trade and American slavery both got their start in New England, while the American abolition movement was born in Dixie. Those who say otherwise are either lying or are ignorant of the facts.

I recommend that anyone with a genuine interest in learning the truth about this subject read my books: *Everything You Were Taught About American Slavery is Wrong, Ask a Southerner!* and *Everything You Were Taught About African-Americans and the Civil War is Wrong, Ask a Southerner!*

ELSTAD: Isn't the Confederate Battle Flag a symbol of slavery and racism?

SEABROOK: The Confederate Battle Flag was not the emblem of the national government of the Confederate States of America. It was the official flag of the Confederate military—which had nothing to do with politics or social institutions. It was only used by Rebel army and navy officers and their soldiers. What does this usage have to do with either slavery or racism?

Even if it had been the official national flag, the C.S.A. wasn't fighting over slavery. It was fighting for constitutional freedom and to protect the lives, homes, and land of its citizens against an aggressive and unwanted intruder.

What the North does not understand, or understands but refuses to honor, is that Southerners have lived under two national flags: the U.S. Flag and the C.S. Flag. Both are important to us here in the South (though for different reasons). In a very real sense, this make Southerners dual citizens of the United States. We are both Unionists (U.S.A.)

This exciting early painting by artist Henry Alexander Ogden, depicts Confederate General Jeb Stuart's raid around Union General George B. McClellan in June 1862.

and Confederates (C.S.A.), and so we have a double allegiance. This is the reality.

The truth is that there have been far more racial crimes committed under the U.S. Flag than the C.S. Flag, and if the Left truly practiced what it preaches, it would ban the former not the latter. We could start with slavery, as just one example. *Every* American slave vessel to ever sail from the U.S. left from Northern ports aboard Northern slave vessels, that were designed by Northern engineers, constructed by Northern shipbuilders, fitted out by Northern riggers, piloted by Northern ship captains, manned by Northern crews, launched from Northern marine ports, funded by Northern businessmen, all which was supported by the vast majority of the anti-abolitionist Northern population. The number of Africans who were abused and who died on these voyages is beyond counting. But we never hear a word from Liberals about taking down the U.S. Flag. Only the C.S. Flag.

But it's really not the flag they hate, is it? It's what it represents: the conservative, Christian, traditional South.

For traditional Southerners the Confederate Battle Flag remains a powerful emblem of our history as a once proud, separate and sovereign country. This sentiment is not going to change now or in the future, and the sooner this is accepted by enemies of the South the better for everyone. For more on the Confederate Battle Flag, see my book *Confederate Flag Facts*.

ELSTAD: Should the South pay some sort of "reparations" to descendants of slaves?

SEABROOK: Why should it when American slavery was launched in the North, the region that practiced slavery far longer than the South and which possessed far more slave owners and slaves than the South well into the early 1800s?

One must also consider that America had thousands of black and Indian slaveholders as well, many who owned not just black slaves, but also white slaves.

Additionally, Portugal introduced African slavery to Europe, Spain introduced it to the Americas, and both the Dutch and the English introduced it to North America. Furthermore, Africa herself was practicing various barbaric forms of slavery on her own people for thousands of years prior to the introduction of the transatlantic slave trade, and indeed was instrumental in opening up and maintaining the slave trade with Arabia and later Europe and America.

Are not all of these regions and nations also culpable? And who is to pay reparations to the modern day descendants of the 1.5 million whites who were held in slavery by Africans in Africa during the late 1700s and early 1800s?

The fact is that because slavery was once a worldwide institution that was found on every continent and among every known people, society, religion, and culture, *all of us descend from both slaves and slave owners.* This makes the idea of *Southern* reparations absurd, meaningless, biased, and illogical.

ELSTAD: Why is Robert E. Lee revered so much in the South? He was a slave owner and just as guilty as everyone else. He swore an oath to the United States of America and violated it. Didn't he deserve what he got?

SEABROOK: More baseless Northern mythology. General Lee was one of the finest examples of American patriotism, authentic Christianity, and Southern traditionalism that this country has ever seen or will ever see. And this is precisely why traditional Southerners *and* enlightened non-Southerners love and honor him.

In Lee's day, while Northerners considered themselves

Big government Liberal, President Abraham Lincoln, meeting with Yankee General George B. McClellan on the field at Antietam, Maryland, 1862. A captured Confederate flag can be seen tossed disrespectfully on the ground to the left. As was the case with so many of Lincoln's military men, he and McClellan did not get along. A Democrat (then the Conservative Party), McClellan had more in common with the Conservative South than the Liberal North. In 1862, after his poor performance at Antietam, Lincoln removed him from his command, further exacerbating an already rancorous relationship. In 1864 McClellan decided to run against Lincoln, a Republican (then the Liberal Party), in November's presidential campaign. The Democrats (Conservatives) wisely called for an immediate halt to the War and a peace treaty with the Confederacy (Conservative), something the Republicans (Liberals) refused to consider at the time. McClellan spoke for many Southerners when he referred to Lincoln as a "well-meaning baboon" and "the original gorilla."

"Americans," our independent-minded Southern ancestors considered themselves "Southerners," freedom-loving men and women who viewed their home state as their true "country." And it was for this reason that when Lincoln decided to invade the South, Lee and millions of other Southerners abandoned the U.S.A. and swore allegiance to their individual states.

And let us note that Lee's decision was not without anguish. He loved the original American government and was loath to renounce it. In the end, after hearing of Lincoln's plans to override the Constitution and undermine the government of the Founding Fathers, he felt he had no choice but to leave the Union in order to fight for their preservation against an enemy hell-bent on obliterating them. To us here in the South, it is not our region that is guilty of "treason," it is the North for seeking to overturn the Ninth and Tenth Amendments.

As for Lee being a "slave owner," no one who has honestly and objectively studied the Lee family would ever make this statement. Unlike Yankee hero Ulysses S. Grant, Lee never personally owned slaves. He did inherit a small group of black servants from his wife Mary Anna Custis, which, upon marriage, she had inherited from her father (as was the custom in both the North and the South at the time).

In addition, General Lee liberated all of the Custis family slaves *before* Lincoln issued his fake and illegal Emancipation Proclamation on January 1, 1863.

Of course, Lee's emancipatory actions are just what one would expect from a Virginian, the state in which the American abolition movement was born.

For more on this fascinating and amazing man, I direct the reader to my books *The Old Rebel: Robert E. Lee As He Was Seen By His Contemporaries*, and *The Quotable Robert E. Lee.*

ELSTAD: Shouldn't all Confederate monuments be taken down?

SEABROOK: As mentioned, Southerners are dual citizens of the U.S. The Southern states once formed their own independent republic, and so we have a different history, with different symbols, different heroes, different stories, different legends, different memories, than the North. Why can this fact not be respected?

It is because the traditional South is largely Christian, constitutionalist, and conservative, things that are detested by many Liberals and nearly all Left-wingers, socialists, Marxists, communists, revolutionaries, and anti-Southers. We say, what does it matter if we have a statue of our greatest leader, President Jefferson Davis, in front of our city hall? Our enemies reply: "Because Davis was a traitor to the U.S. and a racist who owned slaves." To this we say, both secession and slavery were legal at the time. As for the charge of racism, Davis adopted an orphaned black boy (named Jim Limber) during the War, something that white racists simply do not do.

Let's keep in mind that it was Lincoln, not Davis, who repeatedly and publicly called blacks an "inferior race," even referring to them as "niggers" on occasion. And it was Lincoln who, in his Inaugural Address, promised not to interfere with slavery and who was ready to sign the Corwin Amendment (a bill that would have allowed slavery to continue in perpetuity if the Southern states agreed to return to the Union). And it was Lincoln who committed treason when he violated the U.S. Constitution by initiating war without congressional approval.

Using the twisted, intolerant logic of the Liberal Yankee, is it not time to remove all of the statues of Lincoln, erase his face from our money, license plates, and Mount

Three Confederate prisoners at Gettysburg, Pennsylvania, July 1863. Despite their humiliating capture, their faces and body language betray a proud confidence in the moral rightness of the Southern Cause. Learn more about the common Southern serviceman in my book, *Rise Up and Call Them Blessed: Victorian Tributes to the Confederate Soldier, 1861-1901*.

Richmond, Virginia, at War's end in April 1865. For four long years Lincoln cruelly "punished" the South with wholesale destruction, mayhem, and bloodshed. For what? She was only trying to preserve the Constitution and government that had been formed by the Founding Fathers, a unique republic known worldwide as "the Confederate States of America."

Rushmore, and tear down his grotesque Pagan monument in Washington, D.C.? We embrace the Constitution and the First Amendment, and so don't wish to censor our enemies the way they do us. However, if they weren't hypocrites this is exactly what they would do.

Let's be clear. The Southern Confederate States of America was a reality from 1861 to 1865, and countless hundreds of thousands of Southerners died trying to defend it. No amount of persecution, no prohibition, no threats, no laws, no matter how many are passed, will ever eradicate these facts. The C.S.A. is part and parcel of American history, and the people who participated in it—courageous Southern men and women who simply acted on their constitutional rights at the time—as well as their descendants, should be recognized, respected, and honored. Taking away our memorials will never change that.

We will never allow our Confederate forbears to be forgotten. We will never stop honoring them. We will never stop fighting for the Southern Cause. We will never stop celebrating our history. For more on this topic see my book, *Confederate Monuments: Why Every American Should Honor Confederate Soldiers and Their Memorials*.

ELSTAD: The Southern states voluntarily approved the Constitution. What legal standing was there to secede?
SEABROOK: In the mid 1800s the states' rights of both accession (joining the U.S.) and secession (leaving the U.S.) were taken for granted by both the American populace and American statesmen. In fact, secession was the most discussed political concept in America right up to and beyond Lincoln's War. It was so taken for granted that the Founders did not even bother including any obvious reference to it in the

The Union operations against the Confederates at Fort Fisher, North Carolina, December 1864-January 1865, began with a Southern victory and ended with a Southern defeat. Portrayed here is the capture of the Rebel stronghold by Federal forces in mid January.

The principle commanders at the Battle of Corinth, Mississippi, October 4, 1862, were General Earl Van Dorn, C.S.A., and General William S. Rosecrans, U.S.A. Van Dorn was forced to retreat but was not captured, and his men went onto fight another day. Van Dorn himself was not so fortunate. Seven months later, on May 7, 1863, while working at his headquarters in Spring Hill, Tennessee, he was murdered by a jealous husband who suspected him of a dalliance with his wife.

Constitution. Instead, they gave tacit mention of it in the all important Bill of Rights as Amendments Nine and Ten.

While critics of secession decry the actions of the Southern states in 1860 and 1861 as "unconstitutional" and "treasonous," they neglect to mention that there is nothing in the Constitution prohibiting secession. Furthermore, this right was upheld by nearly every member of the Founding Generation, as well as most of our presidents, right up to our fifteenth chief executive, James Buchanan. It was our demagogic sixteenth president, big government Left-winger Abraham Lincoln, who was the first to derail the Constitution, murder countless thousands of Americans, and nearly bankrupt the U.S. Treasury in an attempt to destroy the right of secession. See my book, *All We Ask is to Be Let Alone.*

ELSTAD: The Southern states wanted to control the Union (look at the 3/5 clause in the Constitution as an example). Didn't that give them extra representation in Congress?
SEABROOK: "Control of the Union" was the objective of the North, not the South. During the many congressional squabbles between South and North that preceded Lincoln's War, the South was only seeking to rebalance the scales of power, which had swung over to the Northern side after decades of levying tyrannical policies on Dixie. As for the Three-Fifths Clause, it was an invention of Northerners, not Southerners!

More proof that the Southern states had no interest in "controlling the Union" is the fact that they seceded from it *legally* and *peacefully*; or at least attempted to do so, until they were halted by Lincoln's unwarranted military assault on their new constitutionally formed republic, the Confederate States of America (named after the original name for the United

States of America).

As Southern hero Confederate President Jefferson Davis said at the time:

> In independence we seek no conquest, no aggrandizement, no cession of any kind from the states with which we have lately confederated. All we ask is to be let alone.

This simple request was not honored in Davis' day, and it is still not being honored today.

For more on this topic, see my books *Confederacy 101: Amazing Facts You Never Knew About America's Oldest Political Tradition*; *The Constitution of the Confederate States of America Explained*; and *The Great Yankee Coverup: What the North Doesn't Want You to Know About Lincoln's War!*

ELSTAD: The rise of the KKK is proof that the South hasn't learned it's lesson from the original conflict.

SEABROOK: This question betrays a complete ignorance of both Southern history and American history! What does the KKK have to do with the South, and why are the two so integrally connected in the public mind? Let's examine this for those who are uninformed on the matter.

There were two KKKs in American history. The first I call the "Reconstruction KKK." The second, the "Modern KKK." The Reconstruction KKK lasted only from December 1865 to early 1869, and was a patriotic, pro-Constitution, anti-Yankee, anti-carpetbag organization. Also a social aid and welfare society, the main purposes of this conservative group were to protect those who had been dispossessed by the War, while helping maintain law and order during so-called

A nameless dead Confederate soldier in Virginia in 1864. The North would have you believe that he died fighting to "preserve slavery," something no Southerner would have ever done. The truth is that he perished trying to preserve the Constitution, which Lincoln was determined to overturn.

Confederate prisoners await their fate at a railway depot at Chattanooga, Tennessee, in 1864. Many Rebel soldiers spent the entire War in a Union cell.

"Reconstruction." Not only did the Reconstruction KKK have thousands of black members, there was an all-black KKK chapter in Nashville at one time.

The Modern KKK, created after 1900, has no connection whatsoever to the Reconstruction KKK. The only thing they share in common is their name. Indeed, they are so completely dissimilar in every way that if the modern KKK hadn't borrowed the name of the original (Reconstruction) KKK, no educated individual today would even make any connection between the two.

In my opinion the present day rise of the KKK can be attributed, in large part, to the race-baiting, race merchants who lurk on the extreme Left of the political spectrum. I've been saying for decades, and will continue to say that only racists see racism in everything and everyone, and only racists judge people by the color of their skin. Non-racists, like most traditional Southerners, could care less about skin color and instead judge others by their character.

To any objective person it's obvious that the North is far more racist than the South; and by this I mean not just white racism, but also black and brown racism. This is because racism, among all colors, grows most virulently where liberalism is most strongly established, and in America this is primarily in the Northeast. Notice that all the racial hatred toward white Southerners is flowing from the North southward—not just from blacks, but from Northern whites as well. Isn't that interesting? These are the same people calling our flag a "symbol of hate," an emblem designed around the Christian cross of love!

Actually, you'll see very little hatred of any kind here in Dixie, because we're more accepting of others, and always have been. Early writers, tourists, and foreign visitors to the

The Confederate Capitol at Montgomery, Alabama (now the State Capitol), where Jefferson Davis was sworn in as the first president of the Southern Confederate States of America on February 18, 1861. This building will always be considered a national shrine to traditional Southerners.

The Battle of Fort Henry in western Tennessee took place on February 6, 1862, under the command of Generals Lloyd Tilghman, C.S.A., and Ulysses S. Grant, U.S.A. The severe bombardment of the garrison by Yankee gunboats, under Andrew H. Foote, forced a Confederate surrender. The fall of Fort Henry, along with Fort Donelson ten days later, opened up the Tennessee and Mississippi Rivers to the Union, sealing the doom of the Confederacy.

U.S. made hundreds of remarks about this striking difference between the South and North. Highly educated men, like French diplomat Alexis de Tocqueville, for example, was appalled by the entrenched white racism in the North, and pleasantly surprised by the racial tolerance among whites in the South. This is why the recent resurgence in the KKK is taking place most rapidly outside the South. In fact, since the 1920s, there have always been more KKK chapters and more racial-based hate crimes in the North than in the South. The anti-South movement doesn't want you to know this, so it rewrites history in order to cast the stigma of racism on the South rather the North. But truth cannot be destroyed by editing it or suppressing it—or by openly gaslighting the public. Let's stop associating the South with white racism and the KKK. It's unfair, inaccurate, and unhistorical. For those who want to learn more see my book, *Nathan Bedford Forrest and the Ku Klux Klan: Yankee Myth, Confederate Fact*.

ELSTAD: The North believes that it was justified in trying to free the slaves from an oppressive life, while the South was fighting to keep them in bondage. Wasn't President Lincoln justified then in everything he did to free them?

SEABROOK: 1) The North, where American slavery first took root, did not fight the War to destroy slavery. It fought—according to the many public statements of Lincoln, Grant, the average Union soldier, and even the U.S. Congress—for one sole purpose: to "preserve the Union." As further proof we need only consider the facts that Lincoln promised not to "interfere" with slavery in his Inaugural speech on March 4, 1861, and that the War continued for another two years after he issued his Emancipation Proclamation on January 1, 1863.

2) The South, where the American abolition movement began, did not fight to preserve slavery. It fought—according to the many public statements of Davis, Alexander H. Stephens, the average Rebel soldier, and the Confederate Congress—to "preserve the Constitution of our Revolutionary sires." Confederate General Robert E. Lee said it best:

> All the South has ever desired was that the Union as established by our forefathers should be preserved; and that the government as originally organized should be administered in purity and truth.

3) Though anti-South writers have long cleverly hidden the fact from the public, in his day Lincoln was well-known as a white racist, white supremacist, and white separatist, one who campaigned throughout his entire adult life to have all African-Americans deported (or at least corralled up in their own black-only state); an intolerant Left-wing racial bigot who not only packed his administration and armies with socialists and communists, but who originally wanted to merely stop the spread of slavery, not the institution itself. This is hardly a man that should be called the "Great Emancipator"! This is why, after all, famed former Northern slave Frederick Douglass said that Lincoln's attitude toward blacks lacked "the genuine spark of humanity."

Those who hunger for the truth about Lincoln would do well to consult my books *Abraham Lincoln: The Southern View*; *Lincolnology: The Real Abraham Lincoln Revealed in His Own Words*; *The Unquotable Abraham Lincoln*; *The Unholy Crusade: Lincoln's Legacy of Destruction in the American South*, *The Great Impersonator!: 99 Reasons to Dislike Abraham Lincoln*, and *Lincoln's War: The Real Cause, the Real Winner, the Real Loser*.

An illustration of the short-lived Confederate cabinet. From left to right: Attorney General Judah P. Benjamin, Secretary of the Navy Stephen R. Mallory, Secretary of the Treasury Christopher Memminger (standing), Vice President Alexander Hamilton Stephens, Secretary of War Leroy Pope Walker (standing), President Jefferson Davis, Postmaster John H. Reagan, and Secretary of State Robert Toombs.

At one time the Confederacy was honored even by U.S. presidents. Here Calvin Coolidge hosts a Confederate group outside the White House in December 1927. Thanks to the devilish efforts of the bigoted, liberal, anti-South movement, this is a scene not likely to ever reoccur.

ELSTAD: Is it true that slavery was the cause of the Civil War, as supported by none other than the Confederate States of America Vice President Alexander H. Stephens?

SEABROOK: Like all the other Southern leaders, Stephens said the opposite, that the South fought to "render our liberties and institutions more secure" by "rescuing, restoring, and re-establishing the Constitution." If you're referring to Stephens' "Cornerstone speech," here are the facts.

1) In that address (given March 21, 1861, at Savannah, Georgia), it's held that he made the statement that the

> cornerstone [of the Constitution of the Southern Confederacy] rests upon the great truth, that the negro is not equal to the white man; that slavery . . . is his natural and normal condition.

Were these Stephens' original words? Not according to the speaker himself. Not only was his speech given extemporaneously, but the version of it that has come down to us today is not a literal translation, but a loose "interpretation" of what he said by journalists in the audience. This is why Stephens later repeatedly asserted that his words had been misinterpreted and thus misunderstood.

During his daring raids Confederate Colonel John Singleton Mosby gave the Yankees hell, and he remains one of the South's greatest War heroes. The author descends from the Mosby family.

2) However, even if we take the above quote literally, it is far from what pro-North historians claim it to be. It turns out that it was the North which believed that "slavery is the cornerstone of American society," for Stephens was merely citing the speech of a *Yankee* judge, Associate Justice of the

Peace of the Supreme Court, Henry Baldwin of Connecticut, who, 28 years earlier (in 1833) had said:

> Slavery is the cornerstone of the [U.S.] Constitution. The foundations of the Government are laid and rest on the rights of property in slaves, and the whole structure must fall by disturbing the cornerstone.

3) In the end, as Richard M. Johnson noted in 1884, all Stephens did during his speech was accurately point out the fact that "on the subject of slavery there was no essential change in the new [Southern Confederate] Constitution from the old [U.S. Constitution]."

U.S. rifled cannon being stored at an arsenal yard in Charleston, South Carolina. Only a left-wing dictatorial Yankee with megalomaniacal aspirations would stoop to using weaponry of this sort on fellow Americans, simply for practicing their constitutional rights. His name was Abraham Lincoln, a moniker that will go down in infamy.

4) The final nail in the coffin of this particular Yankee fairy tale is the fact that Stephens was known far and wide as a "true friend of the black man," an epithet that was never once applied to Lincoln while he was alive, and for obvious reasons: this was the same man who referred to blacks as "niggers," detested the abolition movement, implemented extreme racist military policies, supported the 1861 Corwin Amendment, was a lifelong member of the anti-black organization the American Colonization Society, used profits from the Yankee slave trade to fund his war, barred African-Americans from the White House, blocked black suffrage and black citizenship, and used slave labor to finish the Capital dome in Washington.

So what was the true cause of the War? It was merely another chapter, albeit a costly, bloody, and senseless one, in the age old conflict between Southern Conservatism and Northern Liberalism. The former region wanted freedom from government, the latter wanted enslavement to government. In essence, the interfering big government-loving, Constitution-hating progressives in the North simply could not abide the thought of a free South, with its emphasis on small limited government, rugged individualism, capitalism, and personal freedom.

Like all wars, it was also about money, as Lincoln himself admitted on numerous occasions. Once when asked, "why not just let the South go?", Lincoln snapped back:

> If I do that, what will become of my revenue? I might as well shut up housekeeping at once.

These are a facts of history, facts that are easily discoverable by anyone willing to take the time to study 19th-Century American political and military literature.

Let me close my comments on this particular topic with a pertinent quote by Jefferson Davis, who summarized the cause of Lincoln's War this way:

> . . . the war was, on the part of the United States Government, one of aggression and usurpation, and, on the part of the South, was for the defense of an inherent, unalienable right.

What was that right? The right of state sovereignty and self-determination as laid out in the U.S. Constitution.

For additional information on Stephens and Davis, see my books *The Alexander H. Stephens Reader*, *The Quotable Alexander H. Stephens*, and *The Quotable Jefferson Davis*.

ELSTAD: Why is the Old South portrayed as a "racist region"?
SEABROOK: American Liberalism can only thrive if its constituents are made to feel dissatisfied about life in the U.S. Since, thanks to the Constitution, we live in one of the richest, and certainly one of the most egalitarian countries in the world, progressives must fabricate various issues to stir up this discontentment. Among these they have invented "the war against women," "the war between the rich and the poor," and "the war between selfish stone-hearted Conservatives and generous compassionate Liberals," just to name a few. Their favorite fake conflict, however, is "the war between the races."

Gen. August von Willich, one of many communists who served in the Union army under Lincoln.

Race baiting is not new to Liberals. They have been pulling out the race card for decades. One of the first Liberals to engage in the merchandising of bigotry was arch white racist

James Ewell Brown Stuart, more popularly known by his initials, "Jeb," was the second most famous cavalryman after Southern hero Nathan Bedford Forrest. While defending our constitutional freedoms, Stuart was mortally wounded at the Battle of Yellow Tavern, dying on May 12, 1864.

May 1863, Confederate Generals Stonewall Jackson (left) and Robert E. Lee (right) meet for the last time on the field of action. Shortly after, at the Battle of Chancellorsville, Lee scored one of his greatest victories. Jackson, however, was both crippled and mortally wounded. Of the mighty Jackson's death Lee said: "He has lost his left arm, but I have lost my right arm."

Abraham Lincoln, who very intentionally invented an imaginary race war between Southern whites and Southern blacks.

Indeed, this was one of the purposes of his Emancipation Proclamation: to stir up racial animosity in Dixie in order to foment a region-wide "slave insurrection." As the document itself tacitly suggests, he and his administration hoped that this would tear the South apart, and in doing so, undermine Southern society to the point where she would be easier to subdue.

Unfortunately for the Great White Supremacist, not a single race riot occurred in the South during his war. The vast majority of Southern blacks remained loyal and on friendly terms with their owners both during and after the conflict, proving once again, if more proof is needed, that Southern "slavery" was not the cruel and racist institution the North has long claimed it to be.

Though Lincoln died before he could see the disastrous fruits of his war on the Constitution and the American people, the Left-wing, socialist, and communist Yankee politicians who survived him were hellbent on perpetuating his contrived "race war," even without a shred of evidence that such racism existed in the South.

One of the first methods they utilized after Dishonest Abe's death was to send thousands of died-in-the-wool Yankee school teachers to the Southern states. Their purpose? To erode and ultimately destroy traditional Southern culture by "reeducating" Southern children in Northern ways and Northern history.

Part of this deceptive and false curriculum was the teaching that the South was "bad" because it was "built on slavery," and that Southerners were "racist" because they kept slaves. Naturally these unwanted invading "educators" ignored the facts that slavery has been practiced worldwide by all races (and is therefore not an inherently racist institution), that American slavery began in the North, that it was not the South but the North that had been constructed around slavery, and that America possessed thousands of black, brown, and red slave owners before the War.

Without question the most powerful ploy that postbellum Yankee liberals used to continue Lincoln's counterfeit race war was the creation of the Union League or Black Loyal League, as it was called. The alleged purpose of the Northern organization was to help dislocated Southern blacks find housing and jobs, who were typically tempted by U.S. government agents with the insincere offer of "forty acres and a mule."

In reality, few if any of the North's promises ever panned out, including this one: the forthcoming mules were nonexistent and seized Southern land was given mainly to wealthy white Yankee industrialists. Consequently, African-Americans received little help in integrating into postwar America, and—thanks to Yankee interference—an estimated 25 percent of Southern blacks died in the aftermath of the Emancipation Proclamation and Reconstruction.

The truth is that the League was merely a front to conceal the North's numerous anti-South activities, one of which was to inculcate Southern blacks with the notion that their white owners were vicious racists who had been using and abusing them for the past 250 years. Thus, with Dixie now weakened and in tatters, the Union League added bribery and intimidation to its campaign to turn the agricultural religious South into an exact duplicate of the industrial atheistic North. This treacherous Northernization process included

No Northerner would ever want you to see this photograph of two Confederate soldiers, one white, one black, for according to Yankee mythology there was no such thing as a "black Confederate." The truth is that, depending on how one defines a "soldier," between 300,000 and 1 million blacks served in the Confederate armies, five times as many as served in the Union armies. Some 8,000 armed blacks fought in Stonewall Jackson's army alone. See my book, *Heros the Southern Confederacy: The Illustrated Book of Confederate Officials, Soldiers, and Civilians.*

The Battle of Hampton Roads, March 8-9, 1862, in which the ironclads *Merrimac* (Confederate) and the *Monitor* (Union) fought. At this Class B conflict—the first time two ironclads engaged one another in history—the *Merrimac* (also known as the *Virginia*) and the *Monitor* came to a stalemate.

paying blacks to stir up animosity against not only their former owners, but all Southern whites. When that Yankee plan failed, threats of violence were employed against African-Americans (mainly the illiterate) with predictable results: anti-white hate crimes committed by Southern blacks rose precipitously, fueling the development of anti-black sentiment across Dixie.

This so-called "white racism," in turn, was used by the Grant Administration and the Northern press to inflame already existing anti-South prejudices in the Northeast, the fulfillment of part of Lincoln's nefarious "white dream" to divide and conquer America. Incidentally, no mention is ever made that Grant himself was a racist slave owner who, during the War, said that he didn't care about abolition and would rather join the Confederacy than fight to end slavery.

But the Yankees' phony race war was short-lived. With the end of "Reconstruction" in 1877, the removal of the last detested Union soldier from Dixie, and the return of former Confederate politicians to office, Southern race relations reverted to their original mutually respectful and affectionate state.

Just as throughout the antebellum period, the South once again became the least racist region of the country, a status it has retained to this day—despite ongoing attempts by the anti-South movement to portray it otherwise.

The End

SUGGESTED READING
Related Books by Lochlainn Seabrook

Seabrook, Lochlainn. *Carnton Plantation Ghost Stories: True Tales of the Unexplained from Tennessee's Most Haunted Civil War House!* 2005. Franklin, TN, 2016 ed.

———. *Nathan Bedford Forrest: Southern Hero, American Patriot.* 2007. Franklin, TN, 2010 ed.

———. *Abraham Lincoln: The Southern View.* 2007. Franklin, TN: Sea Raven Press, 2013 ed.

———. *The McGavocks of Carnton Plantation: A Southern History - Celebrating One of Dixie's Most Noble Confederate Families and Their Tennessee Home.* 2008. Franklin, TN, 2011 ed.

———. *A Rebel Born: A Defense of Nathan Bedford Forrest.* 2010. Franklin, TN: Sea Raven Press, 2011 ed.

———. *Everything You Were Taught About the Civil War is Wrong, Ask a Southerner!* 2010. Franklin, TN: Sea Raven Press, revised 2019 ed.

———. *The Quotable Jefferson Davis: Selections From the Writings and Speeches of the Confederacy's First President.* Franklin, TN: Sea Raven Press, 2011.

———. *The Quotable Robert E. Lee: Selections From the Writings and Speeches of the South's Most Beloved Civil War General.* Franklin, TN: Sea Raven Press, 2011 Sesquicentennial Civil War Edition.

———. *Lincolnology: The Real Abraham Lincoln Revealed In His Own Words.* Franklin, TN: Sea Raven Press, 2011.

———. *The Unquotable Abraham Lincoln: The President's Quotes They Don't Want You To Know!* Franklin, TN: Sea Raven Press, 2011.

———. *Honest Jeff and Dishonest Abe: A Southern Children's Guide to the Civil War.* Franklin, TN: Sea Raven Press, 2012.

———. *Encyclopedia of the Battle of Franklin - A Comprehensive Guide to the Conflict that Changed the Civil War.* Franklin, TN: Sea Raven Press, 2012.

———. *The Quotable Nathan Bedford Forrest: Selections From the Writings and Speeches of the Confederacy's Most Brilliant Cavalryman.* Spring Hill, TN: Sea Raven Press, 2012.

———. *Forrest! 99 Reasons to Love Nathan Bedford Forrest.* Spring Hill, TN: Sea Raven Press, 2012.

———. *Give 'Em Hell Boys! The Complete Military Correspondence of Nathan Bedford Forrest.* Spring Hill, TN: Sea Raven Press, 2012.

———. *The Constitution of the Confederate States of America Explained: A Clause-by-Clause Study of the South's Magna Carta.* Spring Hill, TN: Sea Raven Press, 2012 Sesquicentennial Civil War Edition.

———. *The Great Impersonator: 99 Reasons to Dislike Abraham Lincoln.* Spring Hill, TN: Sea Raven Press, 2012.

———. *The Old Rebel: Robert E. Lee As He Was Seen By His Contemporaries.* Spring Hill, TN: Sea Raven Press, 2012 Sesquicentennial Civil War Edition.

———. *The Quotable Stonewall Jackson: Selections From the Writings and Speeches of the South's Most Famous General.* Spring Hill, TN: Sea Raven Press, 2012 Sesquicentennial Civil War Edition.

———. *Saddle, Sword, and Gun: A Biography of Nathan Bedford Forrest for Teens.* Spring Hill,

TN: Sea Raven Press, 2013.

———. *The Alexander H. Stephens Reader: Excerpts From the Works of a Confederate Founding Father*. Spring Hill, TN: Sea Raven Press, 2013.

———. *The Quotable Alexander H. Stephens: Selections From the Writings and Speeches of the Confederacy's First Vice President*. Spring Hill, TN: Sea Raven Press, 2013 Sesquicentennial Civil War Edition.

———. *Give This Book to a Yankee! A Southern Guide to the Civil War for Northerners*. Spring Hill, TN: Sea Raven Press, 2014.

———. *The Articles of Confederation Explained: A Clause-by-Clause Study of America's First Constitution*. Spring Hill, TN: Sea Raven Press, 2014.

———. *Confederate Blood and Treasure: An Interview With Lochlainn Seabrook*. Spring Hill, TN: Sea Raven Press, 2015.

———. *Nathan Bedford Forrest and the Battle of Fort Pillow: Yankee Myth, Confederate Fact*. Spring Hill, TN: Sea Raven Press, 2015.

———. *Everything You Were Taught About American Slavery War is Wrong, Ask a Southerner!* Spring Hill, TN: Sea Raven Press, 2015.

———. *Confederacy 101: Amazing Facts You Never Knew About America's Oldest Political Tradition*. Spring Hill, TN: Sea Raven Press, 2015.

———. *The Great Yankee Coverup: What the North Doesn't Want You to Know About Lincoln's War!* Spring Hill, TN: Sea Raven Press, 2015.

———. *Slavery 101: Amazing Facts You Never Knew About America's "Peculiar Institution."* Spring Hill, TN: Sea Raven Press, 2015.

———. *Confederate Flag Facts: What Every American Should Know About Dixie's Southern Cross*. Spring Hill, TN: Sea Raven Press, 2016.

———. *Nathan Bedford Forrest and the Ku Klux Klan: Yankee Myth, Confederate Fact*. Spring Hill, TN: Sea Raven Press, 2016.

———. *Seabrook's Bible Dictionary of Traditional and Mystical Christian Doctrines*. Spring Hill, TN: Sea Raven Press, 2016.

———. *Everything You Were Taught About African-Americans and the Civil War is Wrong, Ask a Southerner!* Spring Hill, TN: Sea Raven Press, 2016.

———. *Nathan Bedford Forrest and African-Americans: Yankee Myth, Confederate Fact*. Spring Hill, TN: Sea Raven Press, 2016.

———. *Women in Gray: A Tribute to the Ladies Who Supported the Southern Confederacy*. Spring Hill, TN: Sea Raven Press, 2016.

———. *Lincoln's War: The Real Cause, the Real Winner, the Real Loser*. Spring Hill, TN: Sea Raven Press, 2016.

———. *The Unholy Crusade: Lincoln's Legacy of Destruction in the American South*. Spring Hill, TN: Sea Raven Press, 2017.

———. *Abraham Lincoln Was a Liberal, Jefferson Davis Was a Conservative: The Missing Key to Understanding the American Civil War*. Spring Hill, TN: Sea Raven Press, 2017.

———. *All We Ask is to be Let Alone: The Southern Secession Fact Book*. Spring Hill, TN: Sea Raven Press, 2017.

———. *The Ultimate Civil War Quiz Book: How Much Do You Really Know About America's Most Misunderstood Conflict?* Spring Hill, TN: Sea Raven Press, 2017.

———. *Rise Up and Call Them Blessed: Victorian Tributes to the Confederate Soldier, 1861-1901*. Spring Hill, TN: Sea Raven Press, 2017.

———. *Victorian Confederate Poetry: The Southern Cause in Verse, 1861-1901*. Spring Hill, TN: Sea Raven Press, 2018.
———. *Confederate Monuments: Why Every American Should Honor Confederate Soldiers and Their Memorials*. Spring Hill, TN: Sea Raven Press, 2018.
———. *The God of War: Nathan Bedford Forrest as He Was Seen by His Contemporaries*. Spring Hill, TN: Sea Raven Press, 2018.
———. *The Battle of Spring Hill: Recollections of Confederate and Union Soldiers*. Spring Hill, TN: Sea Raven Press, 2018.
———. *I Rode With Forrest! Confederate Soldiers Who Served With the World's Greatest Cavalry Leader*. Spring Hill, TN: Sea Raven Press, 2018.
———. *The Battle of Nashville: Recollections of Confederate and Union Soldiers*. Spring Hill, TN: Sea Raven Press, 2018.
———. *The Battle of Franklin: Recollections of Confederate and Union Soldiers*. Spring Hill, TN: Sea Raven Press, 2018.
———. *A Rebel Born: The Screenplay* (for the film). Written 2011. Franklin, TN: Sea Raven Press, 2020.
———. (ed.) *A Short History of the Confederate States of America* (Jefferson Davis, Belford Company, NY, 1890). A Sea Raven Press Reprint. Spring Hill, TN: Sea Raven Press, 2020.
———. (ed.) *Prison Life of Jefferson Davis: Embracing Details and Incidents in his Captivity, With Conversations on Topics of Public Interest* (John J. Craven, Sampson, Low, Son, and Marston, London, UK, 1866). A Sea Raven Press Reprint. Spring Hill, TN: Sea Raven Press, 2020.
———. *What the Confederate Flag Means to Me: Americans Speak Out in Defense of Southern Honor, Heritage, and History*. Spring Hill, TN: Sea Raven Press, 2021.
———. *Heroes of the Southern Confederacy: The Illustrated Book of Confederate Officials, Soldiers, and Civilians*. Spring Hill, TN: Sea Raven Press, 2021.
———. *Support Your Local Confederate: Wit and Humor in the Southern Confederacy*. Spring Hill, TN: Sea Raven Press, 2021.
———. *America's Three Constitutions: Complete Texts of the Articles of Confederation, Constitution of the United States of America, and Constitution of the Confederate States of America*. Spring Hill, TN: Sea Raven Press, 2021.
———. *Vintage Southern Cookbook: 2,000 Delicious Dishes From Dixie*. Spring Hill, TN: Sea Raven Press, 2021.
———. *The Bittersweet Bond: Race Relations in the Old South as Described by White and Black Southerners*. Spring Hill, TN: Sea Raven Press, 2022.

The South's most beloved general, Robert Edward Lee.

MEET THE INTERVIEWEE

NEO-VICTORIAN SCHOLAR LOCHLAINN SEABROOK, a descendant of the families of Alexander Hamilton Stephens, John Singleton Mosby, Edmund Winchester Rucker, and William Giles Harding, is a 7th generation Kentuckian and one of the most prolific and widely read writers in the world today. Known by literary critics as the "new Shelby Foote" and the "American Robert Graves," and by his fans as the "Voice of the Traditional South," he is a recipient of the United Daughters of the Confederacy's prestigious Jefferson Davis Historical Gold Medal. As a lifelong writer he has authored and edited books ranging in topics from history, politics, science, religion, astronomy, military, and biography, to nature, music, humor, gastronomy, alternative health, genealogy, and the paranormal; books that his readers describe as "game changers," "transformative," and "life altering."

One of the world's most popular living historians, he is a 17th generation Southerner of Appalachian heritage who descends from dozens of patriotic Revolutionary War soldiers and Confederate soldiers from Kentucky, Tennessee, North Carolina, and Virginia. Also a history, wildlife, and nature preservationist, he began life as a child prodigy, later transforming into an archetypal Renaissance Man. Besides being an accomplished and well respected author-historian and Bible authority, he is also a Kentucky Colonel, eagle scout, screenwriter, nature, wildlife, and landscape photographer, artist, graphic designer, songwriter (3,000 songs), film composer, multi-instrument musician, vocalist, session player, music producer, genealogist, former history museum docent, and a former ranch hand, zookeeper, and wrangler.

Currently Seabrook is the author and editor of nearly 100 adult and children's books (containing a total of some 25,3500 pages and 12,700,900 words) that have earned him accolades from around the globe. His works, which have sold on every continent except Antarctica, have introduced hundreds of thousands to vital facts that have been left out of our mainstream books. He has been endorsed internationally by leading experts, museum curators, award-winning historians, bestselling authors, celebrities, filmmakers, noted scientists, well regarded educators, TV show hosts and producers, renowned military artists, illustrious religious leaders, esteemed heritage organizations, and distinguished academicians of all races, creeds, and colors.

Of northern, western, and central European ancestry, he is the 6th great-grandson of the Earl of Oxford and a descendant of European royalty through his Kentucky father and West Virginia mother. His modern day cousins include: Johnny Cash, Elvis Presley, Lisa Marie Presley, Billy Ray and Miley Cyrus, Patty Loveless, Tim McGraw, Lee Ann Womack, Dolly Parton, Pat Boone, Naomi, Wynonna, and Ashley Judd, Ricky Skaggs, the Sunshine Sisters, Martha Carson, Chet Atkins, Patrick J. Buchanan, Cindy Crawford, Bertram Thomas Combs (Kentucky's 50th governor), Edith Bolling (second wife of President Woodrow Wilson), Andy Griffith, Riley Keough, George C. Scott, Robert Duvall, Reese Witherspoon, Lee Marvin, Rebecca Gayheart, and Tom Cruise.

A constitutionalist, avid outdoorsman, and gun rights advocate, Seabrook is the author of the international blockbuster, *Everything You Were Taught About the Civil War is Wrong, Ask a Southerner!* He lives with his wife and family in beautiful historic Middle Tennessee, the heart of the Old South.

For more information on author Mr. Seabrook visit
LOCHLAINNSEABROOK.COM

Confederate General Thomas "Stonewall" Jackson, a cousin of the author, at the Battle of First Manassas ("Bull Run" to Yanks), August 17, 1861. Jackson was one of the most adulated generals of the Confederacy, and for good reason: an authoritative but flexible officer, his good-natured Christian personality and numerous quirks and eccentricities endeared him to his soldiers and his fellow commanders, both on and off the field. He perished May 10, 1863, from a wound suffered at the Battle of Chancellorsville, where he was hit by friendly fire, one of the greatest Southern losses of the War. Like most of the Confederate brass, Jackson was a non-slave owner (the few servants he had under his roof requested to live with him, or were given to him due to his kindness) who fought for the preservation of the Constitution, not slavery, as the anti-South movement falsely asserts. A man who actually practiced Jesus' commandment to "love everyone," in 1855 he opened a Sunday school for blacks in Lexington, Virginia, which he paid for with his own money. One of his most memorable statements was made on the battlefield: "Men, draw your swords and throw away your scabbards." Jackson was a true Southerner, one who well earned his place in the Confederate Pantheon of immortal heroes. I selected the painting above for the cover of my book, *The Quotable Stonewall Jackson: Selections From the Writings and Speeches of the South's Most Famous General.*

If you enjoyed this book you will be interested in Colonel Seabrook's popular related titles:

- ABRAHAM LINCOLN WAS A LIBERAL, JEFFERSON DAVIS WAS A CONSERVATIVE
- EVERYTHING YOU WERE TAUGHT ABOUT THE CIVIL WAR IS WRONG, ASK A SOUTHERNER!
- ALL WE ASK IS TO BE LET ALONE: THE SOUTHERN SECESSION FACT BOOK
- EVERYTHING YOU WERE TAUGHT ABOUT AMERICAN SLAVERY IS WRONG, ASK A SOUTHERNER!
- CONFEDERATE FLAG FACTS: WHAT EVERY AMERICAN SHOULD KNOW ABOUT DIXIE'S SOUTHERN CROSS
- LINCOLN'S WAR: THE REAL CAUSE, THE REAL WINNER, THE REAL LOSER

Available from Sea Raven Press and wherever fine books are sold

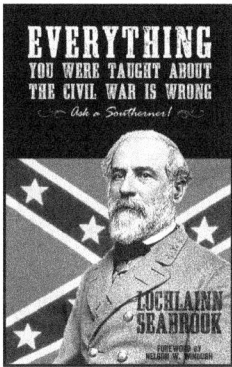
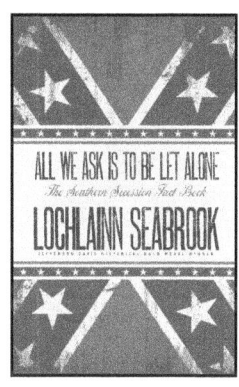

ALL OF OUR BOOK COVERS ARE AVAILABLE AS 11" X 17" COLOR POSTERS, SUITABLE FOR FRAMING

SeaRavenPress.com

www.ingramcontent.com/pod-product-compliance
Lightning Source LLC
Chambersburg PA
CBHW061345040426
42444CB00011B/3092